BOOK TWO

31 SELECTED DUETS

FOR TWO CLARINETS

(Intermediate – Advanced)

Compiled and Edited by

JAY ARNOLD

Advancing from Book One, consisting of 50 Selected Duets for Two Clarinets in easy to intermediate form, we now present 31 Selected Duets for Two Clarinets by masters in this form of composition, with arrangements of an intermediate to advanced grade. These duets will be of great value to the repertoires of players who have acquired proficiency in the intermediate grades.

CONTENTS

FIFTEEN DUETS

By Various Composers

JACQUES FEREOL MAZAS

Moderato con moto

1

4

FRANCESCO GEMINIANI

Allegretto

2

6

RONDO
Allegretto

MICHEL J. GEBAUER

3

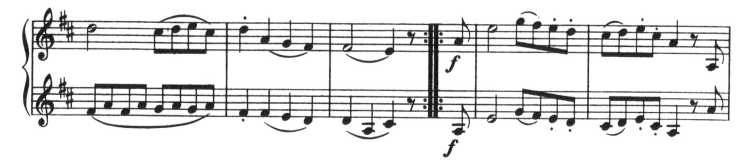

JOSEPH HAYDN

Menuetto

Trio

FRANCESCO GEMINIANI

BARTOLOMEO CAMPAGNOLI

ANTONIO B. BRUNI

7

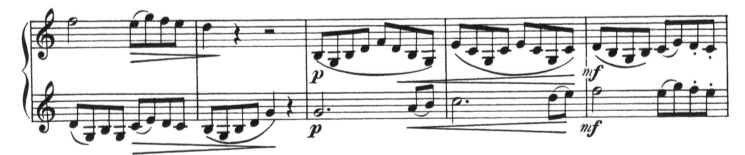

Allegretto ma non troppo

JACQUES FEREOL MAZAS

8

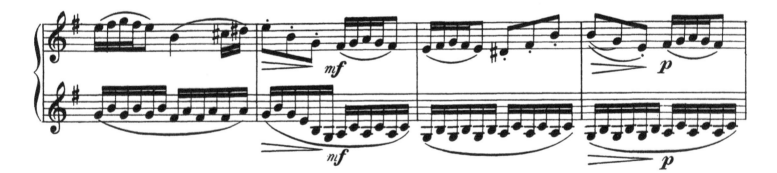

GIOVANNI BATTISTA VIOTTI

Menuetto

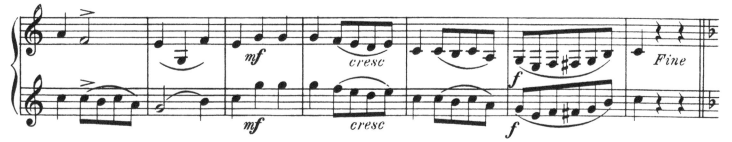

RONDO
Allegretto

JACQUES FEREOL MAZAS

10

JACQUES FEREOL MAZAS

11

JACQUES FEREOL MAZAS

Andante

12

RONDO
Allegro non troppo

IGNAZ JOSEPH PLEYEL

13

THEME AND VARIATIONS

W. A. MOZART

Andantino grazioso

14

VAR. 1

VAR. 2

VAR. 3
Allegro ma non troppo

Allegro moderato

W. A. MOZART

15

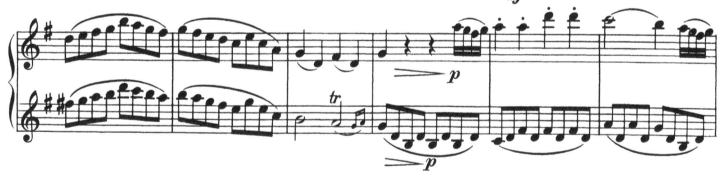

THIRTEEN DUETS

AURELIO MAGNANI

Andante sostenuto

2

con passione

f   *f*

animando un poco   *affrettando*

rall.   **A tempo**

Allegretto scherzoso

Moderato

Andantino con moto

5

Tempo di Gavotta

7

ROMANCE

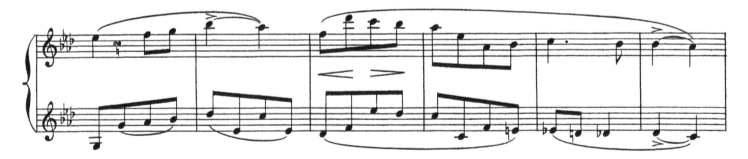

SARABANDE

Un poco più mosso

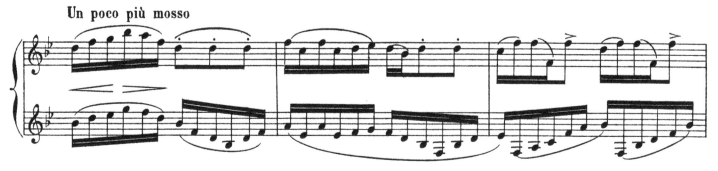

I.º Tempo

pp *tranquillamente*

ritard - - *p* a Tempo

p

SCHERZO
In A Minor

MINUET

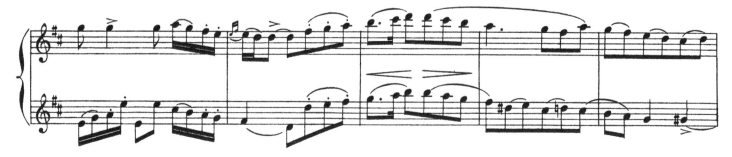

LARGO APPASSIONATO

Largo assai

13

THREE DUETS
From Opus 94

OVERTURE

ROBERT KIETZER

Allegro molto M.M. (♩ = 120)

Allegro molto M.M. (♩ = 120)

ROMANCE

CAPRICE

3

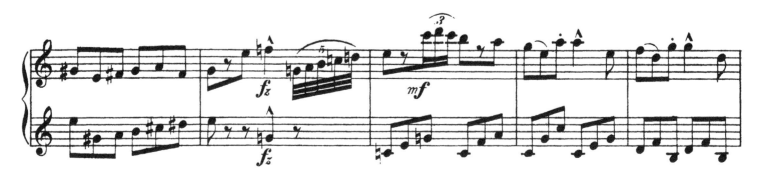